rain + bow = rainbow

Amanda Rondeau

Consulting Editor Monica Marx, M.A./Reading Specialist

ABDO
Publishing Company

Published by SandCastle™, an imprint of ABDO Publishing Company, 4940 Viking Drive, Edina, Minnesota 55435.

Printed in the United States.

Credits
Edited by: Pam Price
Curriculum Coordinator: Nancy Tuminelly
Cover and Interior Design and Production: Mighty Media
Photo Credits: Comstock, Corbis Images, Digital Vision, Eyewire Images, Hemera, Carey Molter, PhotoDisc, Stockbyte

Library of Congress Cataloging-in-Publication Data

Rondeau, Amanda, 1974-
    Rain + bow = rainbow / Amanda Rondeau.
        p. cm. -- (Compound words)
    Includes index.
    Summary: Illustrations and easy-to-read text introduce compound words related to nature and being outdoors.
    ISBN 1-59197-436-4
    1. English language--Compound words--Juvenile literature. [1. English language--Compound words.] I. Title: Rain plus bow equals rainbow. II. Title.

PE1175.R6675 2003
428.1--dc21

                                                                    2003048155

SandCastle™ books are created by a professional team of educators, reading specialists, and content developers around five essential components that include phonemic awareness, phonics, vocabulary, text comprehension, and fluency. All books are written, reviewed, and leveled for guided reading, early intervention reading, and Accelerated Reader® programs and designed for use in shared, guided, and independent reading and writing activities to support a balanced approach to literacy instruction.

Let Us Know

After reading the book, SandCastle would like you to tell us your stories about reading. What is your favorite page? Was there something hard that you needed help with? Share the ups and downs of learning to read. We want to hear from you! To get posted on the ABDO Publishing Company Web site, send us e-mail at:

sandcastle@abdopub.com

SandCastle Level: Transitional

sun + flower =

rainbow

A rainbow has many colors.

It looks pretty in the sky.

rain + bow =

A compound word is two words joined together to make a new word.

sunflower

Grace and Ryan are looking for seeds in a sunflower.

butter + fly =

butterfly

Claire and her sister are looking at a butterfly.

water + fall =

waterfall

Sam and his family hiked up a hill to see a waterfall.

sun + shine =

sunshine

Erin likes to be outdoors in the sunshine.

summer+time=

summertime

Molly and her friends have a picnic in the summertime.

Joy Follows a Rainbow

There was a field of
sunflowers in Joy's
front yard.

Her mom said she could get lost, so be on guard.

Joy chased a butterfly into the flowers.

She couldn't see
the house and was
lost for hours.

Then a rainbow appeared and showed her the way home.

Now when Joy is outside, she will
no longer roam!

More Compound Words

bluebird	quicksand
buttercup	rainfall
earthquake	redwood
landform	songbird
landslide	sunlight
marshland	thunderstorm
moonlight	tumbleweed
overcast	vineyard

Glossary

butterfly an insect with a slender body and large colorful wings

rainbow an colorful arc in the sky caused by sunlight shining through raindrops or mist

roam to wander around aimlessly

sunflower a tall plant with a large flower that has yellow petals and edible seeds

sunshine the light from the sun

About SandCastle™

A professional team of educators, reading specialists, and content developers created the SandCastle™ series to support young readers as they develop reading skills and strategies and increase their general knowledge. The SandCastle™ series has four levels that correspond to early literacy development in young children. The levels are provided to help teachers and parents select the appropriate books for young readers.

Emerging Readers
(no flags)

Beginning Readers
(1 flag)

Transitional Readers
(2 flags)

Fluent Readers
(3 flags)

These levels are meant only as a guide. All levels are subject to change.

To see a complete list of SandCastle™ books and other nonfiction titles from ABDO Publishing Company, visit **www.abdopub.com** or contact us at:

4940 Viking Drive, Edina, Minnesota 55435 • 1-800-800-1312 • fax: 1-952-831-1632